CELEBRATING THE FAMILY NAME OF WANG

Celebrating the Family Name of Wang

Walter the Educator

Silent King Books
a WhichHead Entertainment Imprint

Copyright © 2024 by Walter the Educator

All rights reserved. No part of this book may be reproduced in any manner whatsoever without written permission except in the case of brief quotations embodied in critical articles and reviews.

First Printing, 2024

Disclaimer

This book is a literary work; the story is not about specific persons, locations, situations, and/or circumstances unless mentioned in a historical context. Any resemblance to real persons, locations, situations, and/or circumstances is coincidental. This book is for entertainment and informational purposes only. The author and publisher offer this information without warranties expressed or implied. No matter the grounds, neither the author nor the publisher will be accountable for any losses, injuries, or other damages caused by the reader's use of this book. The use of this book acknowledges an understanding and acceptance of this disclaimer.

Celebrating the Family Name of Wang is a memory book that belongs to the Celebrating Family Name Book Series by Walter the Educator. Collect them all and more books at WaltertheEducator.com

USE THE EXTRA SPACE TO DOCUMENT YOUR FAMILY MEMORIES THROUGHOUT THE YEARS

WANG

From distant lands where dragons soar,

The name of Wang is steeped in lore.

A heritage both vast and strong,

A family bound by heart and song.

The character strokes, precise and bold,

Tell tales of wisdom, strength untold.

Each line a river, flowing deep,

Through time and trials, their roots do keep.

From scholars' scrolls to farmers' fields,

The name of Wang its power wields.

With steady hands and minds so keen,

They shaped a legacy, proud and serene.

Builders of bridges, thinkers of change,

Explorers of lands both near and strange.

Through centuries past, their spirits remain,

Unyielding through joy, through loss, through gain.

In courts of kings or village square,

The Wangs have left their imprint there.

A tapestry of deeds they weave,

Of honor earned and dreams achieved.

The winds of history call their name,

A family steeped in timeless fame.

Their bond unbroken, their path aligned,

A shining star through endless time.

With every dawn, the name inspires,

A spark to kindle ancient fires.

In every heart, their story lives,

A beacon bright, a light that gives.

Through storms they've sailed, through peace they've stayed,

In every era, the course they've laid.

From humble roots to heights unknown,

The Wang name stands, a tower of stone.

A legacy of courage and might,

Guided by wisdom, crowned by light.

Through generations, their spirit rings,

The Wang name soars on eagle's wings.

So let us raise a song of pride,

For all the Wangs, past and present, worldwide.

A family timeless, steadfast, and true,

Their name, a treasure ever renewed.

ABOUT THE CREATOR

Walter the Educator is one of the pseudonyms for Walter Anderson. Formally educated in Chemistry, Business, and Education, he is an educator, an author, a diverse entrepreneur, and he is the son of a disabled war veteran. "Walter the Educator" shares his time between educating and creating. He holds interests and owns several creative projects that entertain, enlighten, enhance, and educate, hoping to inspire and motivate you. Follow, find new works, and stay up to date with Walter the Educator™

at WaltertheEducator.com

www.ingramcontent.com/pod-product-compliance
Lightning Source LLC
LaVergne TN
LVHW052009060526
838201LV00059B/3927